Theme 4

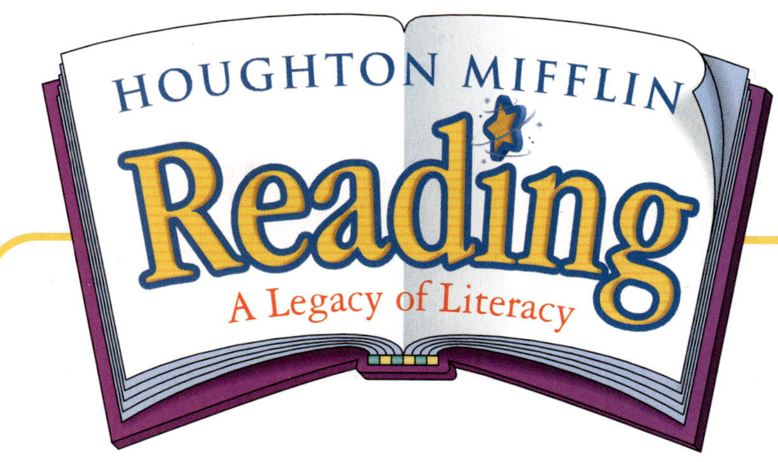

Amazing Animals

HOUGHTON MIFFLIN BOSTON • MORRIS PLAINS, NJ

California • Colorado • Georgia • Illinois • New Jersey • Texas

Printed in the U.S.A.

ISBN 0-618-16210-0

456789-BS-07 06 05 04 03 02

Design, Art Management, and Page Production: Silver Editions.

Contents

A Park for Parkdale

by Patty Moynahan
illustrated by Bethann Thornburgh

Parkdale is a very nice town. It has houses and farms and stores. It has a market that sells nearly everything. It is a fine town, except for one thing. Parkdale has no park.

At the town meeting, Bart Horn stood up. “I have something important to say this morning,” he told the town board. “We feel that a town named Parkdale needs a park.”

Doctor Short nodded. So did Miss Martin.

“Pardon me,” said Cora Barkway, “but how will we pay for this park? We will need land. We will need someone to tend to this park.”

The people began to think. Then Bart had an idea.

“Listen!” said Bart. “We will work together to make this park.”

The people liked this smart plan.

“We’ll start right now!” said Bart. “I know a good spot for our park.”

Bart led everyone to an old, weedy lot. "Let's make a park!" he shouted.

Doctor Short and others cleaned up trash. Miss Martin planted a garden. More and more people came to help.

On March first, Parkdale Park opened. People ate and played and had fun. The mayor made a speech.

He said, “We are proud. See what can happen when everyone helps out!”

Parkdale is a very nice town. It has houses and farms and stores and a market.

And now it has a park!

Arthur's Book

by Patty Moynahan
illustrated by John Manders

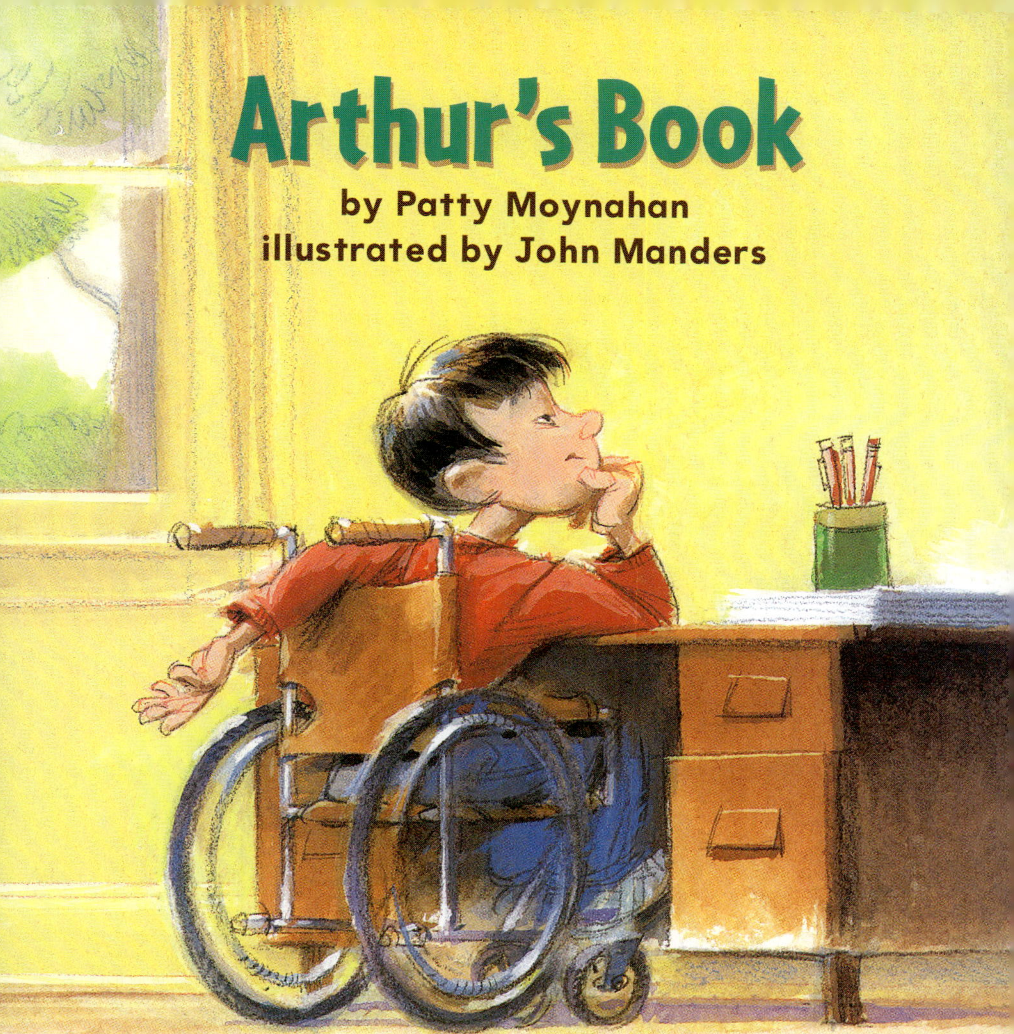

Arthur wanted to write his own book. He had stacks and stacks of nice white paper. He had three new pens. He had lots of time for writing. Just one thing was missing.

Arthur needed an idea. He started thinking and thinking.

"I'll tell a tale about a frightful sea creature," he told himself. "It could be a mixture of fact and fiction."

Arthur looked out the window. He saw his cat chasing his dog.

"How will this sea creature act?" he asked. "That's the question."

Arthur kept thinking and thinking.

Outside, his dog jumped up a tree. Arthur did not see.

"My brain is starting to hurt," said Arthur. "How hard can it be to get an idea?"

Then Arthur looked back outside. He saw his cat run up the tree. He saw his dog in the tree. It was very funny.

"Sea creatures do not do funny things like that!" Arthur said. "I need a new idea."

Arthur felt that it might be helpful to look at books. He picked up a book from the fiction section of his shelf. Just then, his dog and cat raced by. They made him drop his book. That got his attention.

"That's it!" he yelled. He had an idea.

"My story will be about a cat that chases a dog. I know about that!" he said.

Then he went back to his desk and started to write.

Hank's Pandas

by Linda Dunlap
illustrated by Teri Sloat

My big brother is named Hank. He takes care of pandas at Animal Park. Hank tells me stories about his work. If I want, he takes me to see his pandas.

Hank begins his work day by feeding the pandas. Zoo pandas eat foods that wild pandas eat. They chomp on plants.

Then Hank might weigh the new baby. It is so small! Hank can hold it in his arms.

Between his chores, Hank just watches the pandas. He likes to think and learn about pandas. Hank tells me what he sees.

Mom and her baby drink pond water.
Dad sits close by.

Pandas have nice fur. They groom it every day. Their light parts look as clean as snow.

Mom cleans baby panda. Dad lends a hand. Then they go to sleep.

Hank and I go away quietly. We will be back to see the pandas soon.

Marta's Larks

by Linda Dunlap

Illustrated by Christiane Beauregard

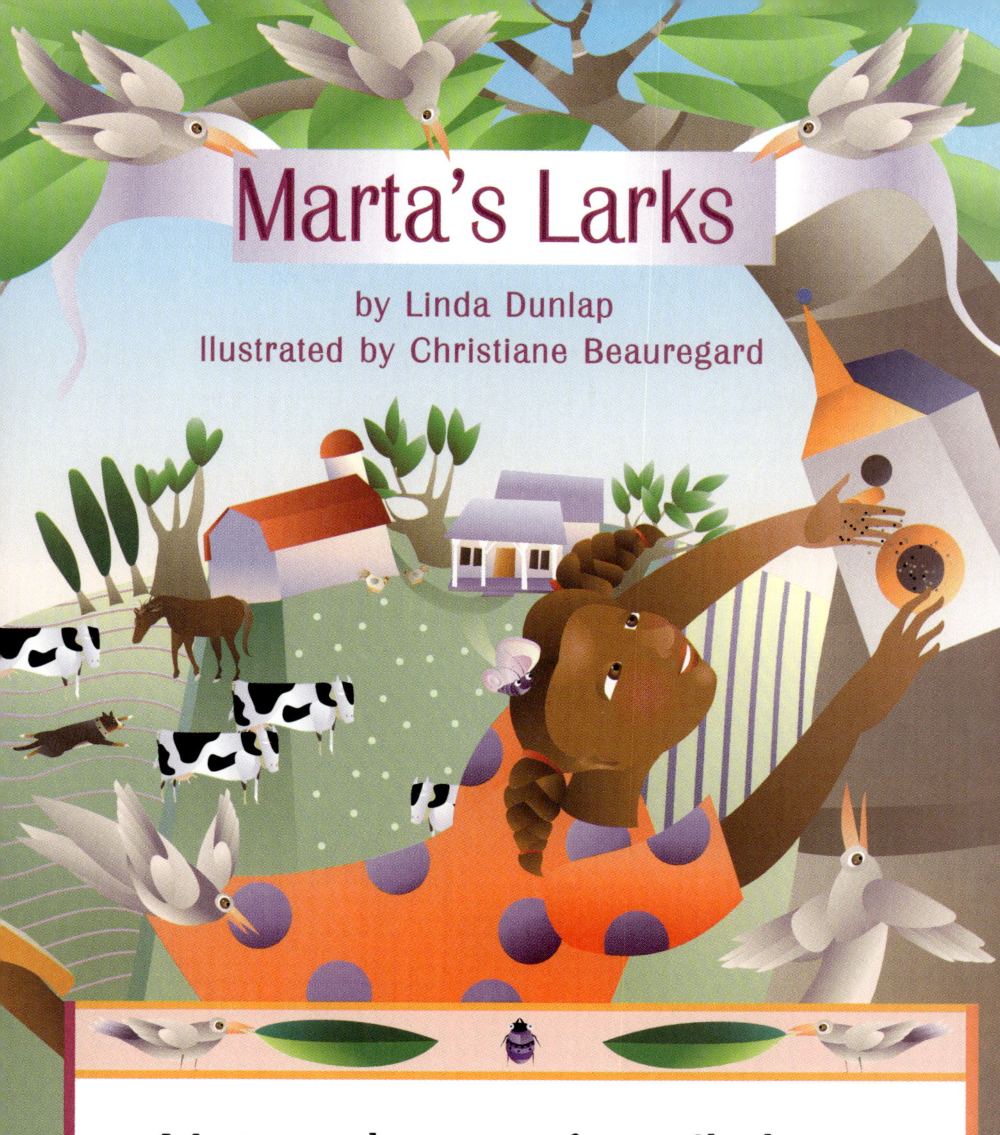

Marta was born on a farm. She has chores every day. The chore she likes best is feeding larks. Larks are birds that sing a lot. Marta likes to hear them each day.

In March, Marta works in her garden. She sees larks try teamwork to turn a leaf. "What is under that leaf?" Marta thinks.

Marta picks up the leaf. A fat bug looks back at her! "Wow! Those larks are smart!" exclaims Marta. "I will start watching larks at work."

Marta sees larks working hard finding food. Even little larks eat lots of bugs. Larks swoop and dart in the sky. Hardly any bugs get away!

Marta sees larks working hard making nests. Larks pull bits of bark from large trees. They take blades of grass from the yard. Larks find torn yarn. They carry these things to a safe place. Then larks turn bark, grass, and yarn into nests!

Marta likes watching larks at work. And larks feel safe when Marta is close. Marta would never harm her larks!

Marta is a part of her larks' life. Larks perch on her arms. Others eat seeds from her hands. Marta is glad to have larks for friends.

Crow's Plan

by Melissa Blackwell Burke
illustrated by Cary Phillips

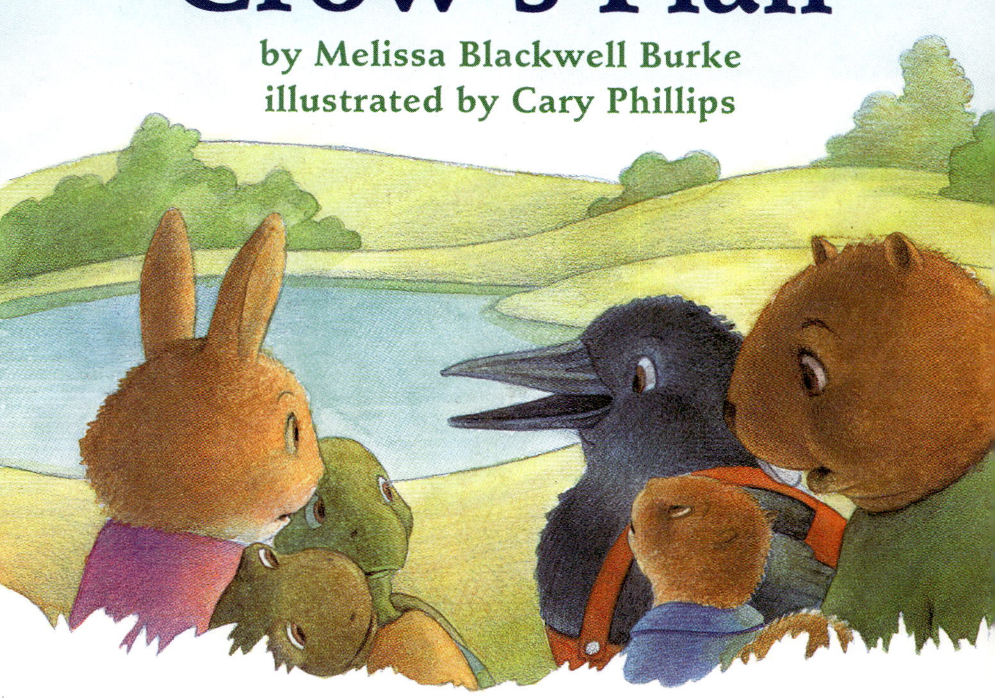

The animals at Oak Lake had a big problem. They met in the field to speak about it.

"Long ago, Oak Lake flowed clean," said Crow. "Now trash floats in it. We must make this lake flow clean once more."

"How can we help?" Toad croaked.

"We will make war on trash. Follow me!" said Crow.

Half the animals went around one side of Oak Lake. The rest went around the other side. They picked up trash and put it in trash cans.

“This lake looks good and clean,” Toad croaked. “Let’s keep it this way.”

“We can wait in this hollow tree,” Crow said. “Then we will show everyone how to take care of the lake. It must be our goal.”

Soon a raccoon family came to Oak Lake. The family ate a picnic in their rowboat. When they finished, the little raccoon tossed something. In a flash, Crow dove and got that trash in his beak before it hit Oak Lake.

Crow dropped that trash in a trash can. He flew back and bellowed at that family.

"I think I know why Crow is mad," the dad explained. "We won't throw trash again, fellow," he yelled up at Crow.

Crow went back to the hollow tree and spoke with the animals. “This is how we will show everyone. It must be our goal.”

“Yes,” they said. “You have our oath. If we see someone throw trash, we will croak or moan or bellow.”

So when you hear animals croak or moan or bellow, think about this tale. And don't throw trash!

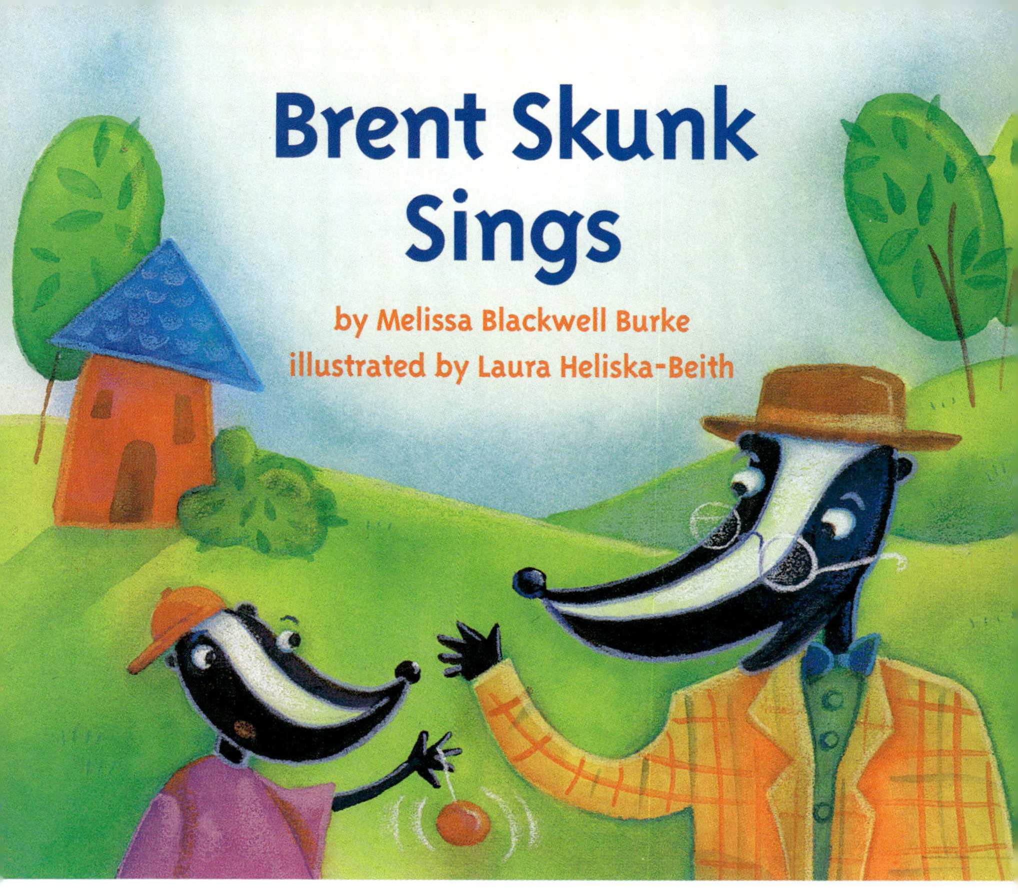

Brent Skunk Sings

by Melissa Blackwell Burke

illustrated by Laura Heliska-Beith

It was time for Brent Skunk to make his first trip to the dentist.

"This bird is the best dentist in this land," Granddad Frank said. "He is quite nice. When we go, he will clean your teeth and check them out. It will not hurt a bit."

Brent Skunk was afraid.

"This dentist visit won't take long," Granddad Frank said. "And you can bring that yo-yo you like so much."

So Brent Skunk and Granddad Frank went down to the dentist.

Brent Skunk and Granddad Frank sat in the waiting room.

When it was time to see the dentist, Granddad Frank found Brent Skunk behind a plant.

Granddad Frank yanked Brent Skunk out.

Granddad Frank set Brent Skunk down. Brent Skunk slumped.

Just then, the dentist came in.

"Brent Skunk, you'll be fine. We'll just count and clean and check those teeth. Let me get my lamp on so we can see. Open wide, please."

But Brent Skunk kept his mouth closed tight. He just sat there blinking.

"We'll get you a new toy with a string when we are through," the dentist said. "Now please open up."

Brent Skunk still kept his mouth closed tight.

“This skunk has me stumped!” the dentist said. “What do you think we can try, Frank?”

“He opens wide when he laughs. We need to make him laugh. Can you do a stunt with that yo-yo?” Granddad Frank asked.

The dentist did three stunts. And Brent Skunk laughed, but with his hand over his mouth.

“I’ve got it!” Granddad Frank said. “Brent can’t pass up a chance to sing. How about it, Brent?”

So Brent Skunk sang, and opened wide.

The dentist counted and cleaned and checked Brent’s teeth.

It did not hurt a bit.

Word List

Theme 4

A Park for Parkdale **(p. 1)** accompanies *Officer Buckle and Gloria.*

DECODABLE WORDS

Target Skills

_r_-Controlled Vowel _ar_

Barkway, Bart, farms, garden, March, market, Martin, pardon, park, Parkdale, smart, start

_r_-Controlled Vowels _or, ore_

Cora, Doctor, for, Horn, important, mayor, more, morning, Short, stores

Words Using Previously Taught Skills

an, and, at, ate, but, came, can, cleaned, did, everything, except, feel, fine, first, fun, good, had, happen, has, he, help, helps, houses, how, is, it, know, land, led, let's, liked, lot, made, make, me, meeting, Miss, named, need, needs, nice, no, nodded, now, on, opened, out, pay, plan, planted, played, proud, right, say, see, sells, shouted, so, speech, spot, stood, tend, that, then, thing, think, this, town, trash, up, we, weedy, we'll, when, will

HIGH-FREQUENCY WORDS

New

board, listen, told

Previously Taught

a, are, began, everyone, have, I, idea, nearly, old, one, opened, others, our, people, said, someone, something, the, to, together, very, what, work

Arthur's Book **(p. 9)** accompanies Officer *Buckle and Gloria.*

DECODABLE WORDS

Target Skill (Review)

Common Syllables *–tion, –ture*

attention, fiction, section, creature, creatures, mixture

Words Using Previously Taught Skills

about, act, an, and, Arthur, asked, at, back, be, book, books, brain, by, can, cat, chases, chasing, desk, did, dog, drop, fact, felt, for, frightful, from, funny, get, got, had, hard, he, helpful, him, himself, his, how, hurt, in, is, it, jumped, just, kept, know, look, looked, lots, made, might, missing, my, need, needed, new, out, outside, own, not, pens, picked, question, raced, run, saw, sea, see, shelf, stacks, started, starting, story, tale, tell, that, that's, then, thing, things, thinking, this, three, time, tree, up, went, white, will, write, writing, yelled

HIGH-FREQUENCY WORDS

Previously Taught

a, could, do, I, idea, of, one, paper, said, the, they, to, told, very, wanted, was

Hank's Pandas (p. 17) accompanies *Ant.*

DECODABLE WORDS

Target Skills

Words with *nd, nt, mp, ng, nk*

chomp, drink, hand, Hank, Hank's, kingdom, lends, panda, pandas, plants, pond

Base Words and Endings *-s, -es, -ies*

chores, foods, parts, sees, stories, takes, tells

Words Using Previously Taught Skills

and, animal, arms, as, at, away, baby, back, be, big, by, can, clean, cleans, close, dad, day, eat, feeding, for, fur, go, groom, he, her, his, if, in, is, it, just, light, likes, look, me, might, mom, my, named, new, nice, on, park, quietly, see, sits, sleep, snow, so, soon, that, then, tree, we, wild, will, with, zoo

HIGH-FREQUENCY WORDS

New

between, care, weigh

Previously Taught

a, about, begins, brother, every, have, hold, I, learn, small, the, their, they, think, to, want, watches, water, what, work

Marta's Larks **(p. 25)** accompanies *Ant.*

DECODABLE WORDS

Target Skill (Review)

r*-Controlled Vowels *-ar, -or, -ore

arms, bark, born, chore, chores, dart, farm, garden, hard, hardly, harm, large, larks, larks', March, Marta, Marta's, part, smart, start, torn, yard, yarn

Words Using Previously Taught Skills

and, at, ate, back, best, big, birds, bits, blades, bug, bugs, by, close, day, each, eat, every, exclaims, fat, feeding, feel, felt, find, finding, food, for, from, get, glad, grass, hands, her, in, is, leaf, likes, looks, lot, lots, making, nests, on, perch, picks, place, safe, seeds, sees, she, sky, swoop, take, that, them, then, these, things, thinks, those, trees, try, turn, up, when, will, wow

HIGH-FREQUENCY WORDS

Previously Taught

a, any, are, away, even, friends, has, have, hear, I, into, little, never, of, others, pull, the, they, to, under, was, watching, what, work, works, working, would

Crow's Plan (p. 33) accompanies *The Great Ball Game.*

DECODABLE WORDS

Target Skill

Vowel Pairs *oa, ow*

bellow, bellowed, croak, croaked, Crow, fellow, floats, flow, flowed, follow, goal, hollow, know, moan, Oak, oath, rowboat, show, slow, throw, Toad

Words Using Previously Taught Skills

about, and, animals, around, at, ate, be, before, big, back, beak, came, can, cans, care, carry, clean, dad, don't, dove, dropped, everyone, family, finished, flash, flew, for, good, got, had, he, help, his, hit, how, if, in, is, it, keep, lake, let's, little, looks, mad, make, me, met, more, must, my, now, on, other, picked, picnic, problem, put, raccoon, rest, saw, see, side, so, soon, speak, spoke, take, tale, that, this, then, think, tossed, trash, tree, up, wait, way, we, went, when, why, will, with, won't, yelled, yes, you

HIGH-FREQUENCY WORDS

New

ago, field, half, war

Previously Taught

a, about, again, have, hear, I, long, of, once, one, or, our, said, the, their, they, to

Brent Skunk Sings **(p. 41)** accompanies *The Great Ball Game.*

DECODABLE WORDS

Target Skill (Review)

Words with *nd, nt, mp, ng, nk*

and, behind, blinking, Brent, Brent's, bring, count, counted, dentist, found, Frank, Granddad, hand, lamp, land, plant, sang, sing, Skunk, slumped, string, stumped, stunt, stunts, think, went, yanked

Words Using Previously Taught Skills

about, asked, be, best, bird, bit, but, came, can, can't, chance, check, checked, clean, cleaned, closed, did, down, fine, for, get, go, got, had, has, he, him, his, how, hurt, is, it, I've, just, kept, let, like, listen, make, me, mouth, much, my, need, new, nice, not, on, opened, opens, out, over, pass, please, quite, room, sat, set, so, see, still, take, teeth, that, them, then, this, those, three, tight, time, toy, trip, try, up, visit, waiting, we, we'll, when, wide, with, will, won't, you, you'll, yo-yo

HIGH-FREQUENCY WORDS

Previously Taught

a, afraid, are, behind, do, first, in, laugh, laughed, laughs, long, open, said, the, there, through, to, was, what, your

HIGH-FREQUENCY WORDS TAUGHT TO DATE:

Grade 1

a
able
about
above
afraid
after
again
against
all
already
also
always
and
animal
any
are
arms
around
away
baby
bear
because
been
before
began
begin
bird
blue
body
both
break
brown
build
butter
buy
by
call
car
carry
caught
children
cling
cold
color
come
could
cow
dance
divide
do
does
done
door
down
draw
eat
edge
eight
else
enough
evening
ever
every
fall
family
far
father
find
first
five
flower
fly
follow
for
forest
found
four
friend
full
funny
garden
girl
give
go
goes
gone
good
green
grow
happy
hard
have
he
head
hear
her
here
hold
horse
house
how
hungry
hurt
I
idea
in
is
jump
kind
know
laugh
learn
light
like
little
live
long
look
love
many
me
minute
more
morning
most
mother
my
near
never
not
now
ocean
of
off
old
on
once
one
only
open
or
other
our
out
over
own
paper
part
people
person
picture
piece
play
present
pretty
pull
put
read
ready
right
room
said
saw
school
second
see
seven
shall
sharp
she
shoe(s)
shout
show
sing
small
so
some
soon
start
sure
table
talk
tall
teacher
the
their
there
these
they
thought
three
through
tiny
to
today
together
too
try
turn
two
under
upon
very
walk
wall
want
warm
was
wash
watched
water
we
wear
were
what
where
who
why
work
world
would
write
you
your

Grade 2

across
ago
beautiful
behind
believe
between
board
bought
brother
brought
busy
care
clothes
different
during
even
field
floor
front
great
guess
half
heard
important
kitchen
lady
later
letter
lion
listen
move
order
poor
quiet
reason
roll
soldier
special
stand
story
straight
surprise
told
touch
until
war
weigh
whole
winter
word
year
young

Decoding Skills Taught to Date: Short Vowels *a, i;* Base Words and Endings *–s, -ed, -ing;* Short Vowels *o, u, e;* Structural Analysis: VCCV Pattern; Long Vowels *a, i* (CVC*e*); Long Vowels *o, u, e* (CVC*e*); Two Sounds for *g;* Consonant Clusters *r, l, s;* Two Sounds for *c;* Double Consonants; Structural Analysis: VCV Pattern; Consonant Digraphs *th, wh, sh, ch, (tch);* Base Words and Endings *–er, -est;* Vowel Pairs *ai, ay;* Compound Words; Vowel Pairs *ow, ou;* Suffixes *–ly, -ful;* Vowel Pairs *ee, ea;* Common Syllables *–tion, –ture; r*-Controlled Vowels *ar, or, ore;* Words with *nd, nt, mp, ng, nk;* Base Words and Endings *-s, -es, -ies;* Vowel Pairs *oa, ow*